Letterland™

Lift-the-flap

WHO'S THAT?

Katie Carr

Collins Educational

An imprint of HarperCollins*Publishers*

cake

camera

candle

castle

Who's that creeping under the mat?
A little mouse ...

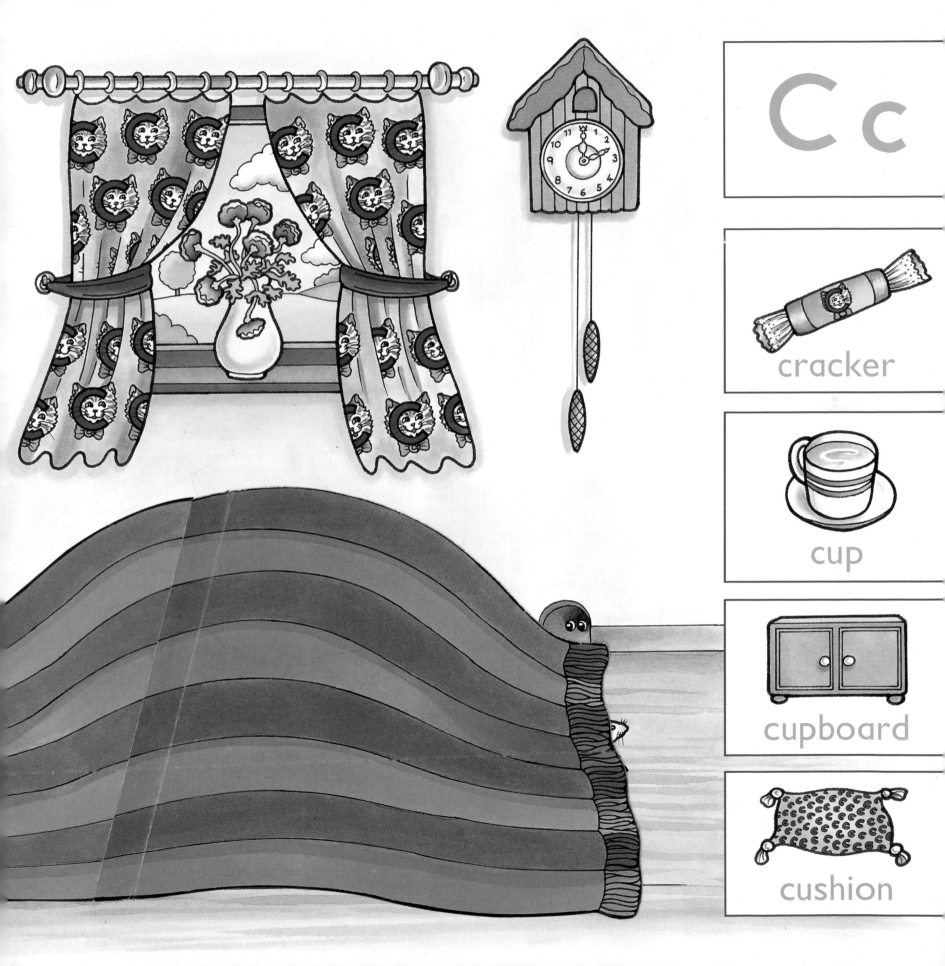

C c

cracker

cup

cupboard

cushion

Who's that driving his yellow van?
Where are you going ...

yacht

yak

yellow

y y

yoghurt

egg yolk

yo-yo

K k

kangaroo

key

king

Who's that coming on stage to sing?
Let's all clap ...

K k

kite

kittens

koala

B b

ball

bee

bluebell

boat

Who's that counting up to ten?
Come and find us …

B b

bridge

bush

buttercup

butterfly

R

rabbit

radio

rake

recorder

Who's that sneaking inside the shed?
What *are* you doing ...

R r

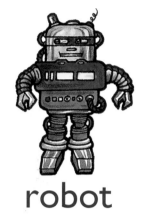

robot

rope

rose

ruby ring

S s

sandwiches

sausages

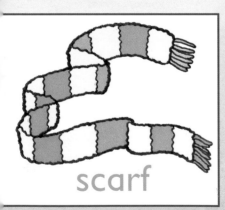

scarf

scissors

Who's that with a slice of cake?
Happy Birthday ...

Birthday

S s

spoons

strawberries

straws

streamers

Who's that going for a swim?
That was a big splash ...

jacket

jam

jeans

jeep

J j

jelly

jet

juice

jumper

M m

magpie

map

menu

monkey

Who's that munching on a bike?
Maybe it's a monster! It's only …

M m

motorbike

mountain

mouse

mushrooms

Menu
mushrooms
Marshmallows
Melon
Motorbike!

Who's that dancing to the band?

banjo

drum

flute

guitar

recorder

trumpet

violin

HERE ARE SOME MORE LETTERLAND TITLES ...

... FOR YOU TO ENJOY

The Letterland alphabet is the basis of the well-known Letterland system for the teaching of reading used in the majority of English primary schools.